W9-AOX-683

★ SPORTS HEROES ★
CHAD OCHOCINCO

Sloan MacRae

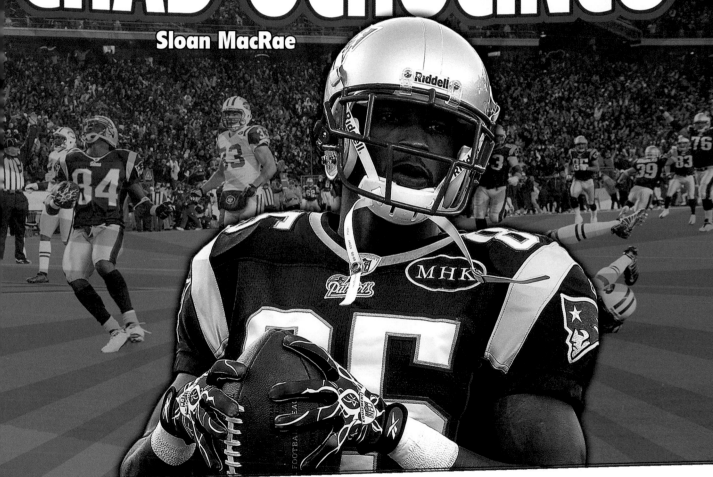

PowerKiDS
press™

New York

Published in 2012 by The Rosen Publishing Group, Inc.
29 East 21st Street, New York, NY 10010

First Edition

Editor: Jennifer Way
Book Design: Julio Gil

Photo Credits: Cover (main) Jim Rogash/Getty Images; cover (background) Rob Tringali/SportsChrome/Getty Images; pp. 4–5 Jim Davis/The Boston Globe via Getty Images; p. 6 Scott Boehm/Getty Images; p. 7 Jamie Squire/Getty Images; p. 8 Joe Robbins/Getty Images; p. 9 Streeter Lecka/Getty Images; p. 10 Stephen Dunn/Allsport/Getty Images; p. 11 Jeff Gross/Getty Images; p. 12 George Gojkovich/Getty Images; pp. 13, 17 (right), 18 Andy Lyons/Getty Images; pp. 14–15 Kirby Lee/Getty Images; p. 16 Rick Stewart/Getty Images; p. 17 (left) Heinz Kluetmeier/Sports Illustrated/Getty Images; p. 19 Kevin Winter/Getty Images; p. 20 Stephen Cohen/WireImage for GQ Magazine/Getty Images; p. 21 Alberto E. Rodriguez/Getty Images for Children Mending Hearts; p. 22 Marc Serota/Getty Images.

Library of Congress Cataloging-in-Publication Data

MacRae, Sloan.
 Chad Ochocinco / by Sloan MacRae. — 1st ed.
    p. cm. — (Sports heroes)
 Includes index.
 ISBN 978-1-4488-6162-0 (library binding) — ISBN 978-1-4488-6282-5 (pbk.) — ISBN 978-1-4488-6283-2 (6-pack)
 1. Ochocinco, Chad, 1978–—Juvenile literature. 2. Football players—United States—Biography—Juvenile literature. I. Title.
 GV939.J6125M33 2012
 796.332092—dc23
 [B]
                                        2011022730

Manufactured in the United States of America

CPSIA Compliance Information: Batch #WW12PK: For Further Information contact Rosen Publishing, New York, New York at 1-800-237-9932

 CONTENTS

IT'S JUST A GAME

The National Football League (NFL), the **professional** football league in the United States, is a successful business. Teams make millions of dollars selling their merchandise and tickets to games. Players can make millions of dollars each year. People sometimes forget that football is a game first and foremost. Fortunately, Chad Ochocinco reminds them.

Chad Ochocinco is known for his activities off the field as well as his football skills. Here he is during a game against the San Diego Chargers in 2011.

Ochocinco plays **wide receiver** for the New England Patriots. He practices and plays as hard as any player in the NFL, but he plays football like it is a game. Ochocinco wants football to be fun for him and the fans. He often does crazy and silly things so that fans and **journalists** are always talking about him.

Chad Ochocinco started his life as Chad Johnson. He was born on January 9, 1978, in Miami, Florida. Chad's parents were not around for much of his childhood. His grandparents raised him, and he became very close with his grandmother Bessie. He even used to call her Mama.

Ochocinco still loves to play soccer. In fact, he even tried out for the Sporting Kansas City professional soccer team in 2011.

Chad was great at sports at a very young age. His first love was not football, but soccer. Chad did not like school as much as he liked sports, though. He did not always get good grades. He did not understand that paying attention to schoolwork could help him play college and professional sports.

Ochocinco was a wide receiver for the Cincinnati Bengals. Here you can see him in his place at the front as the team lines up to play against the Pittsburgh Steelers.

STRUGGLING IN SCHOOL

Chad was one of the best **athletes** on his Miami Beach Senior High School football team. Chad knew that if he could get into a college with a good football program, it could put him on the path to play in the NFL. If he played professional football, he would be able to take care of his grandmother Bessie, while playing a sport that he loved.

Steve Smith (left) played football with Chad at Santa Monica College. He went on to play for the Carolina Panthers in the NFL. Here are the two men in 2010.

Chad's grades were too low for him to get into the colleges with the best football programs, though. He went to Langston University, in Oklahoma, in 1996. He did not play football there. He struggled in school, and he had to leave after one year.

T. J. Houshmandzadeh (right) was Ochocinco's teammate on the Bengals until 2008. The two men were also college football teammates at Oregon State. Here they are in 2006.

9

Johnson did not give up on his plan to play college football. In 1997, he entered Santa Monica College in California and played football there. His grades were still bad, so he had to sit out the 1998 season. He made up for it in the following year. Top college **scouts** saw him play, and they liked what they saw.

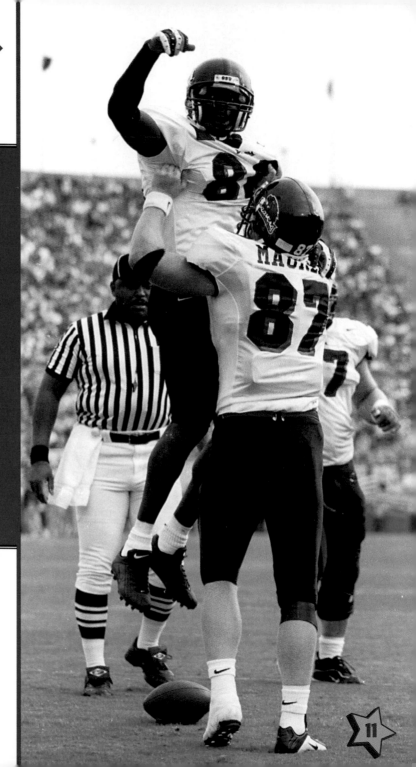

Johnson played so well in his year at Oregon State that he decided to try to move from college football to the NFL. Here he is with Oregon State teammate Martin Mauer (right) in 2000.

In 2000, Johnson **transferred** to Oregon State University, one of the best football schools in the country. He proved himself on the field that year by making some amazing catches. A 97-yard **touchdown pass** against Stanford University made Johnson famous. Now NFL coaches were watching him. Johnson felt ready for the 2001 NFL **Draft**.

During Johnson's year at Oregon State, the team had 11 wins and only 1 loss. They even beat Notre Dame in the 2001 Fiesta Bowl.

THE CINCINNATI BENGALS

The Cincinnati Bengals picked Chad Johnson in the 2001 NFL Draft. The team needed a great player like him. The Bengals had been one of the worst teams in the NFL for several years in a row. They were so bad that even their fans had started calling them the Bungles, because "to bungle" means "to mess up."

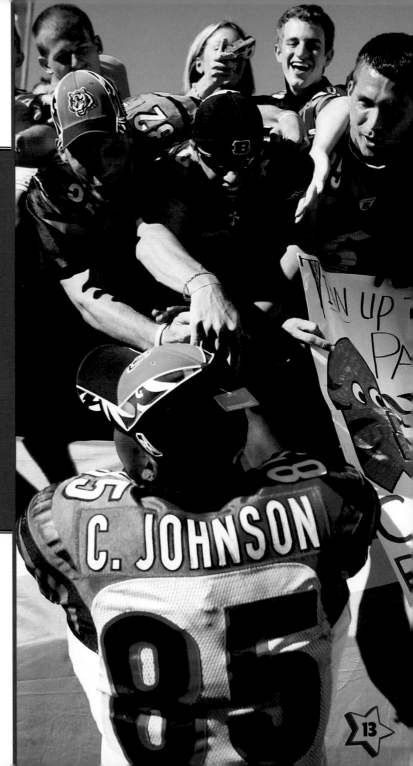

The Cincinnati Bengals' record got better after Johnson joined the team in 2001. This made fans more excited to support the team. Here is Johnson greeting Bengals fans in 2005.

Johnson worked hard to help turn his new team around. Over the next few seasons, the Bengals added more talented players to the team. They drafted a young **quarterback** named Carson Palmer. Palmer and Johnson worked well together. Thanks in part to Johnson, the Bengals were no longer the Bungles.

Ochocinco has set several Bengals records. One of them is for most receptions. A reception is a successful catch.

13

Johnson proved to be one of the best wide receivers in the NFL. Other teams no longer looked forward to playing the Bengals since it would be an easy win! Fans loved watching Johnson make great catches.

Here is Johnson at his second Pro Bowl, in 2004. Football experts, such as coaches and players, vote on who will play in the Pro Bowl. Football fans vote online to pick Pro Bowl players.

Johnson was picked to play in the Pro Bowl in 2003, his third season. The Pro Bowl is a special game at the end of the season. Fans and **experts** pick the best players to play in the bowl. It is like the MLB or NBA All-Star Game. Being picked for the Pro Bowl is an honor that most players only dream about. Ochocinco was picked to play in the Pro Bowl six times in seven years!

BECOMING OCHOCINCO

Here is Johnson during the 2003 season. In this season he set a team record for most receiving yards in a season.

Ochocinco wants football to be fun. Sometimes he does funny dances after making catches. The NFL **fines** players thousands of dollars for fooling around during games. In 2003, Johnson caught a touchdown pass and pulled out a sign that said, "Dear NFL, please don't fine me again." The NFL fined him $10,000.

In 2006, Johnson decided to put the words "Ocho" and "Cinco" on his **jersey** in honor of Hispanic Heritage Month. He wears

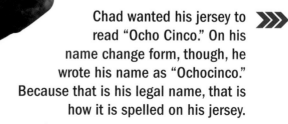

Chad wanted his jersey to read "Ocho Cinco." On his name change form, though, he wrote his name as "Ochocinco." Because that is his legal name, that is how it is spelled on his jersey.

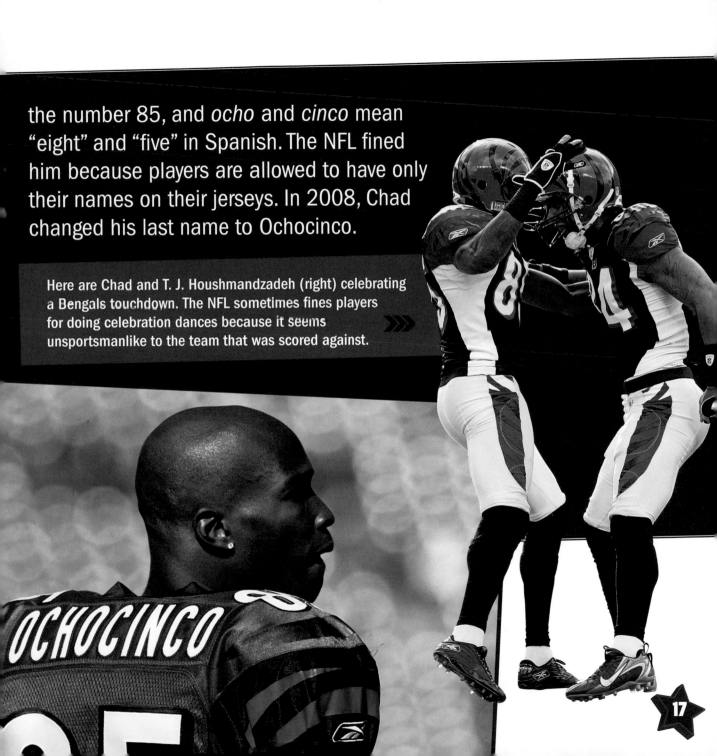

the number 85, and *ocho* and *cinco* mean "eight" and "five" in Spanish. The NFL fined him because players are allowed to have only their names on their jerseys. In 2008, Chad changed his last name to Ochocinco.

Here are Chad and T. J. Houshmandzadeh (right) celebrating a Bengals touchdown. The NFL sometimes fines players for doing celebration dances because it seems unsportsmanlike to the team that was scored against.

NOT JUST FOOTBALL

Ochocinco is as busy off the field as he is in a game. He has starred in several reality television shows, including the tenth season of *Dancing with the Stars*, in which he finished fourth. In 2010, he and his teammate Terrell Owens created a sports TV talk show called *The T.Ocho Show*.

Here is Ochocinco with Cheryl Burke, who was his dance partner on *Dancing with the Stars*. ⟫

In 2011, Ochocinco faced a big change. He was traded to the New England Patriots. Up until then, he had played for the Bengals for all of his professional career. Teammates and fans alike were excited to have Ochocinco bring his athletic talent and his fun-loving personality to his new team.

⟪ Ochocinco (left) and Terrell Owens were Bengals teammates. They are also friends off the field.

Chad has always remembered that his grandmother Bessie helped raise him. He is still close with her today. Ochocinco also has four children. They are named Jicyra, Chade, Cha'ie, and Chad Johnson II. He became engaged to Evelyn Lozada in 2010.

Here are Ruben St. Hilaire (left) and Chad at a 2010 charity event held by Children Mending Hearts. This charity encourages children around the world to work to help others.

Chad works off the field to help those who are not as lucky as he is. A homeless boy named Ruben St. Hilaire wrote Chad a letter saying how much he would like to meet him. Chad invited Ruben to meet lots of famous NFL stars at a football camp. To make it even better, the camp was held on Ruben's birthday!

Here is Chad with his fiancée Evelyn Lozada at a charity bowling event in 2010.

FUN FACTS

>> Ochocinco holds a number of Bengals records, including the most touchdown catches and the most receiving yards of all time.

>> Sometimes Ochocinco sucks his left thumb when he is deep in thought.

>> In 2009, Ochocinco had to fill in as the Bengals' kicker during a game.

>> Chad wrote an autobiography in 2007 called *Ocho Cinco: What Football and Life Have Thrown My Way*.

>> Samari Rolle and Keyshawn Johnson, both football stars, are Chad's cousins.

>> Chad has ridden a bull for charity. He was bucked off in 1.5 seconds. Chad did not ride the bull for long, but he at least tried.

>> Chad Johnson's 2001 97-yard touchdown catch in college is the longest in Oregon State history.

>> Ochocinco is a fan of Oprah Winfrey's.

>> Chad also appeared in a dating show on VH1 called *Ochocinco: The Ultimate Catch*.

>> Chad was in the singer Monica's music video for "Everything to Me."

GLOSSARY

athletes (ATH-leets) People who take part in sports.

draft (DRAFT) The picking of people for a special purpose.

experts (EK-sperts) People who know a lot about a subject.

fines (FYNZ) Makes someone pay money as punishment for breaking a rule.

jersey (JER-zee) A shirt worn as part of a team uniform.

journalists (JER-nul-ists) People who gather and write news for a newspaper or magazine.

professional (pruh-FESH-nul) Having players who are paid.

quarterback (KWAHR-ter-bak) A football player who directs the team's plays.

scouts (SKOWTS) People who help sports teams find new, young players.

touchdown pass (TUCH-down PAS) A pass that lets a teammate score by crossing the other team's goal line in football.

transferred (TRANZ-ferd) Changed schools.

wide receiver (WYD rih-SEE-ver) A football player whose biggest job is to catch passes from the quarterback.

INDEX

WEB SITES

Due to the changing nature of Internet links, PowerKids Press has developed an online list of Web sites related to the subject of this book. This site is updated regularly. Please use this link to access the list:
www.powerkidslinks.com/hero/ocho/